Defending the Military Marriage

By Lt. Col. Jim Fishback, USA (Ret.)
and Bea Fishback

Contents

DEFENDING THE MILITARY MARRIAGE
FamilyLife Publishing®
5800 Ranch Drive
Little Rock, Arkansas 72223
1-800-FL-TODAY · FamilyLife.com
FLTI, d/b/a FamilyLife®, is a ministry of Campus Crusade for Christ
International®

ISBN: 978-1-57229-345-8

Design: Jerry McCall

Printed in the United States of America

16 15 14 13 12   7 8 9 10 11

FAMILYLIFE®
Help for today. Hope for tomorrow.

About the Authors

Lt. Col. Jim Fishback, USA (Ret.) is a graduate of the United States Military Academy at West Point and served with the United States Army for more than 20 years. Jim and Bea were married on October 25, 1975. After retiring in 1994, the Fishbacks joined Campus Crusade for Christ and are currently working in a partnership with the Military Ministry and FamilyLife. Jim and Bea live in the United Kingdom to bring the resources of these ministries to military personnel stationed in Europe and the Middle East. They have two grown children, Jamie and Joni.

Acknowledgments

We would first like to acknowledge Bea's father, Job Doty, who served for five years and was injured three times during World War Two; and Jim's father, Col. Jesse Fishback, USA (Ret.), who served in the Army for 30 years and fought in three wars.

Thanks to our children, Jamie and Joni, who moved many times and lived in three countries during our time in the military.

Thank you to Ken Tuttle, who encouraged us to pursue this study; and to Dave Boehi for guiding and editing this work.

Thanks to our co-laborers in FamilyLife® and the Military Ministry, to our team around the world, and especially to our good friends and mentors, Don and Sue Myers. We would not be here without you.

Finally, we would like to express our gratitude to the men and women who are currently sacrificing in the armed forces so that we may continue to enjoy our freedom.

Jim and Bea Fishback

Before You Begin

Congratulations on deciding to invest your time and energy in your marriage! Participating in this HomeBuilders Couples Series® group will help you build a stronger relationship with your spouse and develop lasting friendships with other couples.

You could complete this study alone with your spouse, but we strongly urge you to either form or join a group of couples studying this material. You will find that the questions in each session help create a special environment of warmth and encouragement as you study together to build the type of marriage you desire.

There are only four ground rules for HomeBuilders group members:

- Share nothing that will embarrass your spouse.
- You may pass on any question.
- Anything shared in the group stays in the group.
- Complete the HomeBuilders Project with your spouse between each session.

May God bless you on your new journey!

Notes To Group Leaders

1. Additional copies of *Defending the Military Marriage* are available for purchase from FamilyLife or from the Military Ministry. To place an order, go to www.FamilyLife.com or call 1-800-FL-TODAY.

2. Leading a group is much easier than you may think! A group leader in a HomeBuilders session is really just a facilitator. As a leader, your goal is simply to guide the group through the discussion questions. You don't need to teach the material—in fact, we don't want you to! The special dynamic of a HomeBuilders group is that couples teach themselves.

3. Be sure to read the Leader's Tips in Appendix B for additional information on
   - leading a session,
   - inviting others to participate in a study,
   - handling childcare,
   - leading a study in your church, and
   - answering the most commonly asked questions about leading a group.

4. Before each session, refer to the Leader's Notes in Appendix C for comments on specific questions in each session.

5. To create an atmosphere that is friendly and comfortable, it is recommended that you do this study in a home setting. In many cases the couple that is leading the study also serves as host to the group. Sometimes involving another couple as host is a good idea. Choose whatever option you feel will work best for your group, taking into account factors such as the number of couples participating and the location.

6. The material presented in each session is designed for a 90-minute study; however, we recommend a two-hour block of time. This will allow you to have time for fellowship and refreshments and still move through each part of the study at a more relaxed pace.

7. It is important to start and end your sessions on time. Also, it is important for couples to commit to attending all four sessions and to completing each of the HomeBuilders projects.

8. *Starting a HomeBuilders Group* is a downloadable resource that provides greater detail on leading a HomeBuilders group available at FamilyLife.com/Resources.

Dear military couples,

When we are married, we make a commitment to "love, honor, and cherish" each other for the rest of our lives. But it usually doesn't take long to discover that building a lasting marriage is a more demanding assignment than we realized it would be!

This is especially true for couples in the military. You face unique challenges that can put tremendous pressure on your love, teamwork, and commitment.

Defending the Military Marriage takes time-tested principles that have helped millions of couples and applies them to the military lifestyle. You will find the study practical, refreshing, and easy to use.

Psalm 127:1a says, "Unless the LORD builds the house, they labor in vain who build it." This study, part of the HomeBuilders Couples Series, will help you apply biblical truths to your marriage. You will learn them in an encouraging environment along with other couples who face the same pressures in marriage.

This is a life-changing tool that will help you build the type of marriage you've always wanted. We hope that this small-group experience will be one of the best experiences of your lives!

Yours for stronger military families,

Dennis Rainey
President
FamilyLife

Jeff Oster
Lieutenant General,
U.S. Marine Corps (Retired)
Interim Executive Directory,
Military Ministry

Basic Training

Learn basic principles that will refresh your
perspective on your marriage mission.

W A R M • U P   15   M I N U T E S

1. Introduce yourself to the group. Share in less than
two minutes (either spouse) how you met.

2. Tell the group how many years you have served in
the military and how many different assignments you've
had.

3. If you could have a "dream" assignment, where
would it be and why?

Military and Marriage

Every marriage relationship is affected by different factors—by the family backgrounds of the husband and the wife, by the choices each has made through the years, by their friends, by their places of employment, etc. As part of the military, you've learned by now that your lifestyle affects your marriage in many unique ways.

1. In what ways can the military lifestyle have a positive influence on a marriage and family?

2. How can the military lifestyle put pressure on a marriage?

Marriage Training Principles

To make a marriage work in the military environment, a couple needs some "basic training" on building a solid marital relationship. For understanding these basics, we are going to turn to what we could call "God's Field Manual for Living"—the Bible.

Let's begin by reading from the creation account in the book of Genesis. After creating man, God decided something was missing:

> Then the LORD God said, "It is not good for the man to be alone; I will make him a helper suitable for him." Out of the ground the LORD God formed every beast of the field and every bird of the sky, and brought them to the man to see what he would call them; and whatever the man called a living creature, that was its name. The man gave names to all the cattle, and to the birds of the sky, and to every beast of the field, but for Adam there was not found a helper suitable for him. So the LORD God caused a deep sleep to fall upon the man, and he slept; then He took one of his ribs and closed up the flesh at that place. The LORD God fashioned into a woman the rib which He had taken from the man, an brought her to the man. The man said, "This is now bone of my bones, and flesh of my flesh; she shall be called Woman, because she was taken out of Man." For this reason a man shall leave his father and his mother, and be joined [cleave] to his wife; and they shall become one flesh. And the man and his wife were both naked and were not ashamed.
>
> Genesis 2:18–25

Training Principle #1: Make Your Marriage Your Priority

3. In this passage God says a husband and wife should leave their parents and "cleave" to their spouses. What do you think it means to "leave" your parents? Why is this important?

4. What types of things in our lives can become a higher priority than our marriage relationship? What happens to the relationship when it doesn't receive enough attention?

Training Principle #2: Build Oneness

5. The passage from Genesis also mentions that a husband and wife "shall become one flesh." Besides the obvious sexual meaning, this means that a man and wife become one emotionally and spiritually as well. "Oneness" in marriage is the total uniting of two lives.

In what ways have you and your spouse grown closer together during the years you have been married? How have you experienced oneness?

Training Principle #3: Make a Lifelong Commitment

Now read Matthew 19:3–6:

> Some Pharisees came to Jesus, testing Him and asking, "Is it lawful for a man to divorce his wife for any reason at all?" And He answered and said, "Have you not read that He who created them from the beginning made them male and female, and said, 'For this reason a man shall leave his father and mother and cleave to his wife, and the two shall become one flesh'? So they are no longer two, but one flesh. What therefore God has joined together, let no man separate."

6. In this passage Jesus says no man should separate what God has joined together. In another passage, Malachi 2:16, God says, "I hate divorce." Why do you think God places such importance on the covenant of marriage?

7. A true lifelong commitment is becoming increasingly rare in our culture. How do you think it helps a marriage when both husband and wife are totally committed to staying together for a lifetime?

HomeBuilders Principle
With the challenges that accompany a military marriage, a couple must decide to make a radical commitment to each other.

We all face different challenges in marriage, but in all these situations we have a choice. We can either use them to draw us closer to each other, or to push us apart. These are choices between oneness and isolation in marriage.

In the remainder of this study we will look at some of the unique issues we face in the military and how we can make choices that build oneness in marriage. One of these common challenges in the military is the Permanent Change of Assignment, the PCS

A PCS in Bible Times

In the Old Testament we find the story of Abram and Sarai, in Genesis 12:1–5:

> Now the LORD said to Abram, "Go forth from your country, and from your relatives and from your father's house, to the land which I will show you; and I will make you a great nation, and I will bless you, and make your name great; and so you shall be a blessing; and I will bless those who bless you, and the one who curses you I will curse. And in you all the families of the earth shall be blessed." So Abram went forth as the LORD had spoken to him; and Lot went with him. Now Abram was seventy-five years old when he departed from Haran. Abram took Sarai his wife and Lot his nephew, and all their possessions which they had accumulated, and the persons which they had acquired in Haran, and they set out for the land of Canaan; thus they came to the land of Canaan.

8. What sacrifices do you think Abram made in obeying God's command?

9. What range of emotions do you think Abram and Sarai experienced as they began their journey? How do you think they dealt with those various emotions?

10. How is the experience of Abram and Sarai similar to the sacrifices a couple will make because of moves while they're in the military? What range of emotions do you face as you prepare for a move?

11. Earlier we talked about three basic training principles for your marriage:

- Make your marriage a priority.
- Build oneness.
- Make a lifelong commitment.

Why do you think these commitments are so crucial to the success of the marriage relationship when couples make a PCS?

1. What is something you've learned during this session that you would like to apply to your marriage relationship?

2. If you can, share with the group any insights you may have discovered.

Make a Date

Make a date with your spouse to meet before the next session to complete the HomeBuilders Project. Your leader will ask you to share something from this experience.

DATE

TIME

LOCATION

Individually:

1. Obviously, no one gets married with the idea of getting a divorce. But what do you think causes couples to begin drifting apart in their relationship?

2. What are some pressures you currently face that, if not addressed, could push you toward isolation in your marriage?

3. Military couples often face unique and stressful situations, due to frequent moves and separations caused by required training or deployment. Therefore, they need to make a conscious decision to recommit themselves to one another and to their marriage.

What does the word "vow" mean to you?

4. When you joined the military, you took a vow that started like this: "I do solemnly swear (or affirm) that I will support and defend the Constitution of the United States against all enemies, foreign and domestic; that I will bear true faith and allegiance to the same . . ."

What would happen to you if you broke this vow in some way?

5. Below is a typical set of marriage vows:

THE MAN: I take this woman to be my lawfully wedded wife. I solemnly promise, before God and these witnesses, that I will love, honor, and cherish her; and that, forsaking all others for her alone, I will perform unto her all the duties that a husband owes to his wife, until God, by death, shall separate us.

THE WOMAN: I take this man to be my lawfully wedded husband. I solemnly promise, before God and these witnesses, that I will love, honor, and cherish him, and that, forsaking all others for him alone, I will perform unto him all the duties that a wife owes to her husband, until God, by death, shall separate us.

What similarities do you see between the vow of allegiance taken when someone joins the military and the vow you take when you join in holy matrimony before God?

4. Read Deuteronomy 23:21–23. How do you think God views a vow taken before Him?

5. In what ways can you continually strive to keep the vows you exchanged in your wedding ceremony?

As a couple:

1. Share your answers from the individual section.

2. Read the wedding vows out loud to one other.

3. Choose two things you will do as a couple during the next week to build oneness in your relationship.

Communicating in the Trenches

Meet each other's needs for communication—even during separations due to temporary deployment.

W A R M • U P   15   M I N U T E S

1. How many separations due to military deployments or training have you experienced since you have been married?

2. In three minutes or less, tell about one funny thing that has happened to you individually or as a family during a deployment or move.

3. If you could pass on one piece of information that you think could be helpful to the other couples in your group in dealing with separations, what would it be?

Separation Blues

Married couples often say that their greatest challenges are in the area of communication. Life in the military can place some unusual pressure on this crucial part of a relationship.

Case Study

"If I have to drag these suitcases out from under the bed one more time so that Steve can go TDY, I think I'll scream," Betty thought to herself as she reached under the bed to retrieve the bags. Wasn't it just yesterday that they had talked about joining the military as an interim job until something else came along? And now here it was, ten years later—ten years with six moves and too many separations to count.

She was surprised to find that she really didn't mind moving so many times. She actually enjoyed seeing new parts of the world, making so many wonderful friends. She was glad their children had a greater understanding of different cultures. She didn't even mind some of the times that Steve had to travel. At first they would act like newlyweds each time he would return. But the "honeymoon" of their reunions ended all too quickly.

Over the last few years the trips came more frequently, and they felt like a greater ordeal than they had in the past. Between keeping up with household responsibilities and caring for three active children between the ages of six and ten, she felt a huge weight of responsibility. And then when Steve returned, just when she desperately needed relief, he always seemed to need a few days to re-adjust to home life and to become involved with the kids again.

On top of that, Betty longed to share with Steve her fears about his recent assignments to dangerous places. She desperately wanted to tell him how worried she was over the friends their children were choosing. She knew they needed to talk more about their finances, about their future. In fact, they needed to discuss a lot of things, but they seemed to talk less and less these days. And now, with Steve about to leave again, the last thing she wanted to do was rock the boat. After all, what if some of these things made him more anxious while he was gone? So, once again, she would say nothing . . . perhaps when he got home from this trip they would take time to talk.

Steve was in the other room working through some last-minute details before heading out the door. He, too, was lost in thought about his upcoming deployment. He wasn't worried about the trip as much as he was concerned about leaving Betty. In the past she had supported his decision to stay in the military, and even encouraged him to put in for advanced training. But lately, she seemed withdrawn and hard to understand.

He wondered if she was beginning to resent all their moves through the years. She always kept up a brave face, but it must hurt to pull up their roots so often.

All he wanted was to take care of his family. He wanted to leave knowing that Betty and the kids were safe, and that they would be here when he returned. He didn't want to have to think about things at home going wrong while he was away.

He was confident that Betty was perfectly capable of handling just about any situation. After all, hadn't she made all the arrangements for their last move while he had gone ahead of the family to his new job? Wasn't she the one who had caused them all to laugh when they discovered that the movers had packed their week-old garbage in their shipment that was heading overseas?

He just didn't want Betty to become too accustomed to his absences. If she did, she might decide she could actually handle things fine without him. Well, he would think about that later. Right now he needed to focus on getting ready to leave.

1. What are some of the issues Betty and Steve were struggling with?

2. Which of those issues have you faced during your years in the military?

3. Why do you think military couples are often hesitant to talk about their concerns before and after separations?

4. If both spouses are on active duty, what other issues might they experience?

5. What do you think might happen to Steve and Betty if they don't resolve these communication issues?

6. What other types of communication problems do you see among couples in the military?

Meeting Your Spouse's Needs

We do not have time in one session to discuss all that the Scripture says about communication in marriage. But we can focus on some biblical principles that will help you deal with the issues military couples face due to frequent or lengthy separations.

7. What are some common themes you find in the following Bible verses?

So, as those who have been chosen of God, holy and beloved, put on a heart of compassion, kindness, humility, gentleness and patience . . .

Colossians 3:12

Therefore if there is any encouragement in Christ, if there is any consolation of love, if there is any fellowship of the Spirit, if any affection and compassion, make my joy complete by being of the same mind, maintaining the same love, united in spirit, intent on one purpose. Do nothing from selfishness or empty conceit, but with humility of mind regard one another as more important than yourselves; do not merely look out for your own personal interests, but also for the interests of others.

Philippians 2:1–4

To sum up, all of you be harmonious, sympathetic, brotherly, kindhearted, and humble in spirit . . .

1 Peter 3:8

Let no unwholesome word proceed from your mouth, but only such a word as is good for edification according to the need of the moment, so that it will give grace to those who hear.

Ephesians 4:29

8. What are some practical ways a married couple could apply these principles . . .

- before a separation?
- during a separation?
- after a separation?

9. Philippians 2:4 instructs us to " . . . not merely look out for your own personal interests, but also for the interests of others." If you were to apply this to your marriage, how could it change the way you look at communicating with your spouse?

Making It Practical

Answer the next two questions with your spouse.

10. Looking back to the Case Study, what could Steve and Betty do to address their communication problems?

11. What could you do to improve your communication in situations like this?

If there is time, report your answers from the last two questions to the group.

WRAP • UP   15 MINUTES

Once a couple recognizes the need for honest, open communication in preparing for a separation, how do you think they can maintain communication during the deployment time? What are some of the ways you have found to successfully do this?

Make a Date

Make a date with your spouse to meet before the next session to complete the HomeBuilders Project. Your leader will ask you to share something from this experience.

DATE

TIME

LOCATION

Individually:

1. Make a list of the different emotional issues that seem to recur as you prepare for separations with your spouse. (For example, what are some fears that you've had?) Try to come up with at least five different issues.

2. After making your list, circle the two issues that you struggle with the most. Pray that God will help you communicate these struggles to your spouse.

3. How do you think your list may differ from the list that your spouse creates? What issue do you think he or she struggles with the most?

4. Many couples have found different ways to stay connected while apart. The following list highlights some ways to combat isolation. In the column that applies to you, put an X in the boxes to indicate the methods you will use to stay in touch with your spouse. Indicate the frequency with which you plan or desire to implement that method.

METHOD	DEPLOYED SPOUSE	SPOUSE AT HOME	FREQUENCY
Phone calls			
E-mail			
Letters			
Skype			
Work through a devotional or HomeBuilders Couples Series® study together			
Cards left with friends to be delivered on key dates			
Arrange for flowers or small gifts			
Put notes inside luggage or hide them at home			
Keep pictures so you and others can see them			
Send home videos to eachother			

Interact as a Couple:

1. Share with each other your answers from questions one through three in the individual section. Be open and understanding as you discuss these issues one at a time.

2. Now that you understand some of the issues your spouse struggles with, what can you do to help meet some of his needs before, during, and after a deployment?

3. After you've done this project, do you have a better understanding of how the military's mobile lifestyle affects your spouse? List how.

4. How will this information help you prepare for the next deployment or separation?

5. Now look at the chart you filled out for question four in the individual section. Make plans for how you intend to stay connected during your next separation.

More-Month-Than-Money Blues

Prioritize financial needs and work through challenges unique to career military families.

W A R M • U P   15   M I N U T E S

"Newlywed Game"

Instruct the husbands to leave the room, and then have the wives answer the following questions on paper. Bring the husbands back and see if they can guess how their wives answered the questions.

1. If you went on a remote assignment for one year and you could only take one personal item with you (excluding family members) what would you take and why? What do you think your spouse would take?

2. Name one special thing you would buy for your spouse if the cost were not an issue. What would your spouse buy for you?

3. What would your spouse say was one thing you learned from the previous Homebuilders Project or the last group session that you would like to start putting into practice in your marriage?

BLUEPRINTS   6o MINUTES

Finances and Isolation

While it's impossible to avoid conflict in marriage—it's inevitable even in the best of relationships—it is possible to learn how to work through it. One of the keys is addressing the source of conflict. Many couples report that financial decisions and pressures spark more conflict than any other issue. This is as true in the military as it is anywhere else, but the military lifestyle includes some unique pressures.

1. From what you've observed, what are some typical challenges military couples have with money, especially during their first years in the service?

2. How can financial struggles cause a couple to experience increased isolation from each other?

3. What do you think can happen in a marriage relationship when one spouse determines to control the financial decisions and leaves the other out?

HomeBuilders Principle
To build oneness in marriage, military couples need to work together to manage their finances.

Scriptural Principles on Handling Money

4. If someone were to examine your checking account and charge card records, what conclusions would he come to about your financial priorities—the most important things to which you allocate money?

5. The Bible includes more than 2,000 verses dealing with money and money management. What do the following passages tell us about what our financial priorities should be?

> *For because of this you also pay taxes, for rulers are servants of God, devoting themselves to this very thing. Render to all what is due them: tax to whom tax is due; custom to whom custom; fear to whom fear; honor to whom honor. Owe nothing to anyone except to love one another; for he who loves his neighbor has fulfilled the law.*
>
> Romans 13:6–8

*But if anyone does not provide for his own, and
especially for those of his household, he has denied the
faith and is worse than an unbeliever.*

1 Timothy 5:8

*Honor the LORD from your wealth and from the first of
all your produce . . .*

Proverbs 3:9

*Go to the ant, O sluggard, observe her ways and be
wise, which, having no chief, officer or ruler, prepares
her food in the summer and gathers her provision in the
harvest. How long will you lie down, O sluggard?
When will you arise from your sleep? . . . Your poverty
will come in like a vagabond and your need like an
armed man.*

Proverbs 6:6–9, 11

6. In what ways can these financial priorities be
undermined by the values and wealth in our culture
today?

7. Borrowing money usually prevents couples from achieving long-term financial success. What are some reasons people give themselves for borrowing money (whether from another person, a lending institution, or a credit card)? Which of those do you think are legitimate reasons for borrowing money?

8. A recent study showed the following statistics about debt and savings in just one of the armed forces:

- Thirty-nine percent of active duty personnel carry a balance from month to month on three or more credit cards.

- Twenty-four percent had personal unsecured debt payments of more than $600 or higher per month.

- Twenty-four percent have monthly payments that are one fourth or more of their monthly income (the national average is 15–20 percent).

- Twenty-eight percent report that they had fallen behind in paying credit card accounts.

- Twenty-four percent have no savings, and twenty-nine percent have savings of less than $1,000.

What do you think causes many military couples today to go so far into debt?

9. What do the following verses have to say about borrowing money?

The wicked borrows and does not pay back, but the righteous is gracious and gives.

Psalm 37:21

The rich rules over the poor, and the borrower becomes the lender's slave.

Proverbs 22:7

Do not be among those who give pledges, among those who become sureties for debts. If you have nothing with which to pay, why should he take your bed from under you?

Proverbs 22:26–27

10. What are some suggestions you would give for staying out of debt?

11. How have you seen couples handle their finances responsibly while still coping with deployments and moves?

12. Read Matthew 6:25–34 (below).

For this reason I say to you, do not be worried about your life, as to what you will eat or what you will drink; nor for your body, as to what you will put on. Is not life more than food, and the body more than clothing? Look at the birds of the air, that they do not sow, nor do they reap nor gather into barns, and yet your heavenly Father feeds them. Are you not worth much more than they? And who of you by being worried can add a single hour to his life? And why are you worried about clothing? Observe how the lilies of the field grow; they do not toil nor do they spin, yet I say to you that not even Solomon in all his glory clothed himself like one of these. But if God so clothes the grass of the field, which is alive today and tomorrow is thrown into the furnace, will He not much more clothe you? You of little faith! Do not worry then, saying, 'What will we eat?' or 'What will we drink?' or 'What will we wear for clothing?' For the Gentiles eagerly seek all these things; for your heavenly Father knows that you need all these things. But seek first His kingdom and His righteousness, and all these things will be added to you. So do not worry about tomorrow; for tomorrow will care for itself. Each day has enough trouble of its own.

Matthew 6:25–34

If you can, tell the group about a time when you trusted God for a financial need, and how He provided.

HomeBuilders Principle
*Military couples can trust that God will provide
for their needs and then learn to live within
His provision.*

W R A P • U P   15 M I N U T E S

1. Answer the following question with your spouse:
What do you think we need to do to begin ordering our
finances around the biblical priorities we've discussed
in this session?

2. If appropriate, share with the group something you
discussed in the previous question with your spouse.

Special Note: Part of the preceding Blueprints content was
adapted by permission from a study in the HomeBuilders
Couples Series®, *Mastering Money in Your Marriage*, by Ron
Blue.

Make a Date

Make a date with your spouse to meet before the next session to complete the HomeBuilders Project. Your leader will ask you to share something from this experience.

DATE

TIME

LOCATION

HOMEBUILDERS PROJECT   6 0   M I N U T E S

Individually:

1. List the financial areas that you think you and your spouse manage well together.

2. List your greatest concerns regarding your personal financial situation.

3. What are some of your financial goals? What would you like your financial situation to be in one year? Five years? Ten years?

4. What first step can you take to accomplish the one-year goal?

As a couple:

1. Share your answers from the individual section.

2. What changes do you need to make in how you manage your finances together so that you can avoid isolation in this area?

3. List one financial decision you are making right now. Share with each other how you would like to manage this.

4. Before deployment, a military couple should put some important financial and legal documents in a safety deposit box or other safe place for easy access for the spouse who is at home. Check the following as an inventory for your personal use and talk about them as a couple:

- A will. (Only 50 percent of all Americans have wills, and most of those are outdated if they have not been reviewed or redone within the past three years.)
- A living trust/will—the legal assistance office can help you make sure your will meets legal standards.
- A record of emergency data, including information about life, health, and car insurance
- A power of attorney document

5. Decide as a couple who will pay the bills and what each of your expenditures will be when you are separated during deployments or temporary duty.

6. Discuss as a couple a time in the next week when you will come together to work on a family budget if you don't already have one in place. Put the time down in your calendar.

7. Close your time in prayer, asking God to give you the wisdom and discipline to handle your finances well.

SEAL Training: SExual Accountability and Love

Recognize the temptations that can threaten your marriage and take positive steps to keep your covenant.

W A R M • U P   15 M I N U T E S

1. Where did you spend your honeymoon, and why did you choose that particular place?

2. What is something funny that happened to you either at your wedding or on your honeymoon? (Remember, don't share anything that will embarrass your spouse!)

3. What is your idea of the perfect date with your spouse?

Common Temptations

Case Study

George lay next to Judy in bed. His long deployment was over. He wasn't sure when he would be traveling again, but for now it was just good to be home. The kids had hung a banner across the front door saying "Welcome Home, Daddy," along with some balloons and confetti. Then a wrestling match of hugs ensued!

After the kids had finally gone to bed, he and Judy had stayed up for hours, talking over things they hadn't discussed in months. When they had finally caught up with how the children were doing, how his trip had been, and how Judy had handled their separation, they experienced an intimacy with each other that he had longed for during their time apart.

He wondered if Judy experienced the same temptations that he faced while he was away. It was so hard to be away from his wife for several months. He was proud that he had never cheated on her, but it wasn't easy. During his time overseas he had ample opportunity to read explicit magazines, be drawn to Internet pornography, watch movies he'd never want his wife to see, and even to dream of other relationships he could have. Sometimes, in his loneliness, he struck up conversations with other women, and on one occasion he had to pull back because he could see that the relationship might become too personal.

Each time he came home to his wife and family, he experienced a level of love that he knew could never be replaced by those other fantasies. But why couldn't he remember that while he was away? What could he do differently the next time he was gone from home to protect his marriage?

Judy smiled and, still half asleep, thought about their reunion. It was so good to have George home. She could relax now and let him handle some of the issues that had arisen while he was away. However, she knew that he couldn't help her handle everything that had gone on while he had been deployed.

She had been so determined not to put herself in a situation that would compromise their marriage. She didn't flirt, and only went out for evenings with friends if she was certain the setting would be safe and neutral. So she was surprised when her temptation came from an unlikely source—a man she had worked with for years. They were working on a project together, and their work often spilled over into long lunches. She enjoyed their conversation; it made her feel attractive to have another man show interest in her.

As the weeks passed during George's absence, she found herself thinking more and more about this man. She realized she didn't know him that well, but she couldn't help comparing him to George. She fantasized about spending more time with him, perhaps on a real date.

Now that George was home, those thoughts seemed hollow and foolish. I'll do better next time George is gone, she promised herself.

1. In what ways were George and Judy putting their relationship in jeopardy during his deployment?

2. What advice would you give each of them about how to protect the sanctity of their marriage?

3. Do you think it is possible to eliminate temptation from your life? If not, how do you think you could reduce temptation in your life?

Protecting Your Marriage

4. What promise do you find in 1 Corinthians 10:13? How could you apply this to your life and marriage? What is an example of a "way of escape"?

> *No temptation has overtaken you but such as is common to man; and God is faithful, who will not allow you to be tempted beyond what you are able, but with the temptation will provide the way of escape also, so that you will be able to endure it.*
>
> 1 Corinthians 10:13

As we look at additional scriptures about temptation, it becomes clear that we need to take two types of actions—offensive and defensive—to protect ourselves from temptation and maintain fidelity in marriage.

5. Read Proverbs 5:18–23:

> ... and rejoice in the wife of your youth. As a loving hind and a graceful doe, let her breasts satisfy you at all times; be exhilarated always with her love. For why should you, my son, be exhilarated with an adulteress, and embrace the bosom of a foreigner? For the ways of a man are before the eyes of the LORD, and He watches all his paths. His own iniquities will capture the wicked, and he will be held with the cords of his sin. He will die for lack of instruction, and in the greatness of his folly he will go astray.
>
> Proverbs 5:18b–23

- Defense: According to this passage, what should motivate us to flee temptation (v. 21–23)?

- Offense: One of the best things you can do is to be exhilarated by the love of your spouse. For many of us, this means rekindling the sparks of romance that can easily begin to grow cool during years of marriage. Turn to your spouse to answer the following question: What are some of the most romantic things we've done to build love in our marriage? Then share one or two of your answers with the group.

6. Read 2 Timothy 2:22:

Now flee from youthful lusts and pursue righteousness, faith, love and peace, with those who call on the Lord from a pure heart.

2 Timothy 2:22

- Defense: What do you think it means to "flee youthful lusts"? How can you apply this principle to some of the temptations you commonly face?

- Offense: What does it mean to "pursue righteousness, faith, love, and peace, with those who call on the Lord from a pure heart"? How can you apply this to your life?

Accountability

Read the following scriptures:

"This is My commandment, that you love one another, just as I have loved you."

John 15:12

Bear one another's burdens, and thereby fulfill the law of Christ.

Galatians 6:2

*Let the word of Christ richly dwell within you, with all
wisdom teaching and admonishing one another with
psalms and hymns and spiritual songs, singing with
thankfulness in your hearts to God.*

Colossians 3:16

*But encourage one another day after day, as long as it
is still called "Today," so that none of you will be
hardened by the deceitfulness of sin.*

Hebrews 3:13

*Therefore, confess your sins to one another, and pray
for one another so that you may be healed. The
effective prayer of a righteous man can accomplish
much.*

James 5:16

7. What do these scriptures say about how we should
relate to one another as Christians?

8. How do you think this type of relationship with other
Christians can help you protect your marriage?

9. In Ephesians 5:21 we are told to "be subject to one another in the fear of Christ." This is the principle of accountability—submitting your life, in the spirit of the scriptures we just examined, to the scrutiny of another person. Accountability means asking another person for advice and spiritual counsel, and giving him (or her) the freedom to make honest observation and evaluations about you.

During deployment or separations an individual should try to establish accountability with others they can trust (never have accountability with a member of the opposite sex). Accountability partners should be able to openly discuss their struggles and temptations with one another. They should be able to ask each other some difficult questions and then pray for one another. The following questions can be used as a guideline:

- Have you struggled with temptation recently? If so, what was the temptation? Be specific.

- Have you been in contact with your spouse while you have been separated? What have you done to keep the lines of communication open? Are you still captivated by her love? Can you be more diligent in this area?

- Have you just lied to me in any of your answers?

How do you think this type of accountability to another Christian, other than your spouse, will help you protect your marriage?

Building a Wall of Protection

10. Turn to your spouse to answer the following: What is one idea we've discussed in this session that we can apply to our marriage in order to build a protective wall around our marriage commitment?

HomeBuilders Principle
We can preserve the sanctity of our marriage commitment by dealing with temptation and by remaining sexually faithful.

As you come to the end of this study, reflect as a group on what you have experienced. Pick one of the following questions to answer and share with the group.

- What has this group meant to you during the course of this study? Be specific.
- What is the most valuable thing you discovered?
- How have you changed as a result of what you've learned in this study?
- What would you like to see happen next for this group?

Make a Date

Make a date with your spouse to meet to complete the HomeBuilders Project.

DATE

TIME

LOCATION

Individually:

1. Review the scriptures we examined during the group session, ending with 1 Corinthians 10:13. Ask God to reveal any areas where you have been dealing with temptation. If necessary, ask for His forgiveness. Thank Him for forgiving you and loving you. Pray that He would give you the strength to protect you from future temptations.

2. Make a list of other men (if you are the husband) or women (if you are the wife) whom you can ask to become "accountability partners" while you and your spouse are separated due to an assignment. This would generally be one or two other people; you would meet with them, discuss areas in which you know you are weak, and agree to answer questions they will ask you. (For example, someone who has trouble avoiding movies with sexual content would have his accountability partner ask specifically if he watched any of these movies during the separation.)

3. Men and women have different emotional and physical needs. What are your physical needs just prior to a deployment? What are your emotional needs? What do you think your spouse's needs are?

4. Sometimes the reunion after a deployment can be just as stressful as it is before the separation. A husband's and wife's needs vary when they are first reunited as a couple and as a family. Compare how your emotional and physical needs are different after a reunion to what they are just prior to the separation. How do you think your spouse's needs differ?

As a couple:

1. Share your answers from the individual time.

2. Affirm your spouse on how he meets your emotional and physical needs. If there are any other ways he can meet your needs, express them in an open, loving manner.

3. Decide on two things you can do as individuals or as a couple to protect your marriage.

4. Close your time in prayer, thanking God for the experience you've had with the HomeBuilders group and for how He has worked in your marriage.

Where Do You Go From Here?

It is our prayer that you have benefited greatly from this study in the HomeBuilders Couples Series®. We hope your marriage will continue to grow as you both submit your lives to God and build your marriage according to His blueprints.

For many of you, a logical next step would be to participate in another HomeBuilders Couple Series study with this group. There are now ten studies in the series, and they cover a variety of topics (see pages 52–53).

If you're interested in staying together as a group, decide:

- When will we begin a new study?

- What study will we use?

- Who will facilitate it?

- Where will we meet?

- Who will order the materials?

We also would like to encourage you to attend a Military Marriage conference or seminar. These weekend conferences will provide an encouraging and intensive opportunity to strengthen your marriage. For more information, contact:

Military Ministry
P.O. Box 120124
Newport News, VA 23612-0124
1-800-444-6006
militaryministry.org

We also hope you will begin reaching out to strengthen other marriages in your community and in your chapel or church. A favorite World War II story illustrates this need clearly:

The year was 1940. The French Army had just collapsed under Hitler's onslaught. The Dutch had folded, overwhelmed by the Nazi regime. The Belgians had surrendered. And the British Army was trapped on the coast of France in the channel port of Dunkirk.

Two hundred and twenty thousand of Britain's finest young men seemed doomed to die, turning the English Channel red with their blood. The Fuehrer's troops, only miles away in the hills of France, didn't realize how close to victory they actually were.

Any rescue seemed feeble and futile in the time remaining. A "thin" British Navy—"the professionals"—told King George VI that at best they could save 17,000 troops. The House of Commons was warned to prepare for "hard and heavy tidings."

Politicians were paralyzed. The king was powerless. And the Allies could only watch as spectators from a distance. Then as the doom of the British Army seemed imminent, a strange fleet appeared on the horizon of the English Channel—the wildest assortment of boats perhaps ever assembled in history. In came trawlers, tugs, scows, fishing sloops, lifeboats, pleasure craft, smacks and coasters, sailboats, even the London fire-brigade flotilla. *Each ship was manned by civilian volunteers—English fathers sailing to rescue Britain's exhausted, bleeding sons.*

William Manchester wrote in his epic book, *The Last Lion,* that even today what happened in 1940 in less than twenty-four hours seems like a miracle—not only were all of the British soldiers rescued, but 118,000 other Allied troops were saved as well.

Today many homes are much like those troops at Dunkirk. Pressured, trapped, and demoralized. We stand waiting for politicians, professionals, even for our pastors and chaplains to step in and save the family. But the problem is much larger than all of those combined can solve.

With the highest divorce rate of any nation on earth, we need an all-out effort by men and women to rescue the exhausted and wounded family casualties. We need an outreach effort by common couples with faith in an uncommon God. For too long, married couples within the church have abdicated the privilege and responsibility of influencing others to those in full-time vocational ministry.

Possibly this study has been used to "light the torch" of your spiritual lives. Perhaps it was already burning, and this provided more fuel. Regardless, may we challenge you to invest your lives in others?

You and other couples around the world can team together to build thousands of marriages and families. By starting a HomeBuilders group, you will not only strengthen other marriages, but you will also see your marriage grow as you share these principles with others.

For more information about HomeBuilders, contact:
FamilyLife
5800 Ranch Dr.
Little Rock, AR 72223
1-800-FL-TODAY, 24 Hours a Day
FamilyLife.com/Resources

The HomeBuilders Couples Series

Building Your Marriage to Last
by Dennis Rainey
(Seven sessions) Learn about and apply God's basic blueprint for a strong, healthy marriage.

Building Teamwork in Your Marriage
by Robert Lewis and David Boehi
(Six sessions) Discover how you are uniquely equipped and that differences are a gift from God.

Growing Together in Christ
by David Sunde
(Six sessions) Unleash power and joy as you and your spouse develop a daily relationship with Christ.

Resolving Conflict in Your Marriage
by Bob and Jan Horner
(Six sessions) Transform conflicts into growth opportunities and grow in love for your spouse.

Mastering Money in Your Marriage
by Ron Blue
(Six sessions) Learn to manage money wisely. Discover how money issues can be a tool for growth and not a root of contention.

Improving Communication in Your Marriage
by Dr. Gary and Barbara Rosberg
((Six sessions) Enhance communication skills and resolve conflict scripturally.

Building up Your Spouse
by Dennis and Barbara Rainey
(Seven sessions) Improve marriage by encouraging and discovering new levels of love and fulfillment.

Managing Pressure in Your Marriage
by Dennis Rainey and Robert Lewis
(Six sessions) Be prepared ... no matter what blows in.

Raising Children of Faith
by Dennis and Barbara Rainey
(Six sessions) Lead children into a relationship with God filled with an understanding of His purpose for them.

Improving Your Parenting
by Dennis and Barbara Rainey
(Six sessions) Strengthen the spiritual foundation in your home by examiningscripture, sharing, and praying together.

Guiding Your Teenagers
by Dennis and Barbara Rainey
(Six sessions) Help your teen make positive memories while resisting unhealthy peer pressure and adolescent traps.

Establishing Effective Discipline for Your Children
by Dennis and Barbara Rainey
(Six sessions) Gain insight on the importance and connection between rules and relationships.

Go to
www.FamilyLife.com/Resources

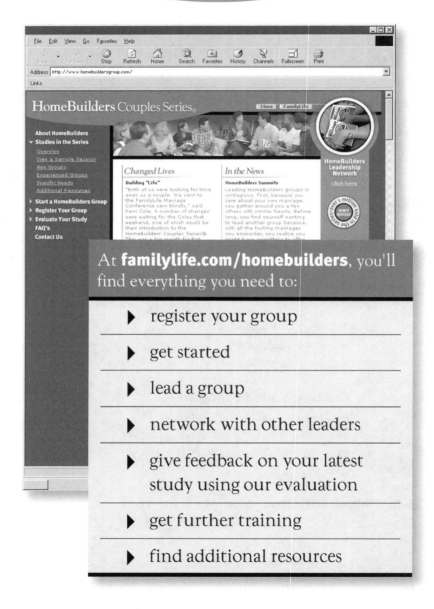

At **familylife.com/homebuilders**, you'll find everything you need to:

- ▶ register your group
- ▶ get started
- ▶ lead a group
- ▶ network with other leaders
- ▶ give feedback on your latest study using our evaluation
- ▶ get further training
- ▶ find additional resources

Connect with other couples today!

Experiencing God's Power

Introduction

- For those who seek it, God provides the power necessary to fulfill His purposes and to carry out His plan for oneness.
- We experience this power by knowing God and by allowing His Spirit to control our lives by faith.

1. God loves you and created you for a relationship with Him.

1. God loves you.

"For God so loved the world, that He gave His only begotten Son, that whoever believes in Him shall not perish, but have eternal life."

John 3:16

2. God wants you to know Him.

"This is eternal life, that they may know You, the only true God, and Jesus Christ whom You have sent."

John 17:3

What prevents us from knowing God personally?

---

2. Humanity is separated from God and cannot know Him personally or experience His love and power.

a. All of us are sinful.

For all have sinned and fall short of the glory of God.

Romans 3:23

b. Our sin separates us from God.

For the wages of sin is death . . .

Romans 6:23a

How can the gulf between God and man be bridged?

3. Jesus Christ is God's only provision for our sin. Through Him alone we can know God personally and experience His love.

a. God became a man in the Person of Jesus Christ.

The Word [Jesus] became flesh, and dwelt among
us, and we saw His glory, glory as of the only
begotten from the Father, full of grace and truth.

John 1:14

b. He died in our place.

But God demonstrates His own love toward us, in
that while we were yet sinners, Christ died for us.

Romans 5:8

c. He rose from the dead.

Christ died for our sins . . . He was buried . . . He
was raised on the third day according to the
Scriptures . . . He appeared to Cephas (Peter), then
to the twelve. After that He appeared to more than
five hundred . . .

1 Corinthians 15:3–6

d. He is the only way to God.

Jesus said to him, "I am the way, and the truth,
and the life; no one comes to the Father, but
through Me."

John 14:6

4. We must individually receive Jesus Christ as Savior and Lord; then we can know God personally and experience His love.

a. We must change our minds about the way we have lived.

b. We must receive Christ by accepting the free gift of salvation He offers us.

But as many as received Him, to them He gave the right to become children of God, even to those who believe in His name.

John 1:12

For by grace you have been saved through faith; and that not of yourselves, it is the gift of God; not as a result of works, so that no one may boast.

Ephesians 2:8–9

Self-Directed Life   Christ-Directed Life

5. What are the results of placing my faith in Jesus Christ? The Bible says:

a. My sins are forgiven. (Colossians 2:13).

b. I possess the gift of eternal life.

And the testimony is this, that God has given us eternal life, and this life is in His Son.

1 John 5:11

c. I have been given the Holy Spirit to empower me to pursue intimacy with God and oneness with my spouse.

6. I can respond to God right now by faith through prayer.

A suggested prayer:

"Lord Jesus, I need You. Thank You for dying on the cross for my sins. I acknowledge that I am a sinner and I am separated from You. Please forgive me. I receive You as my Savior and Lord. Thank You for forgiving my sins and giving me eternal life. Please take control of my life. Make me the kind of person You want me to be."

Signature_____

Date_____

Leader's Tips

The Purpose of *Defending the Military Marriage*

This study is designed to give military couples a tool to help them cope with some of the unique stresses and challenges they face in their marriages. By participating in this study, couples will strengthen their relationships and learn practical steps they can take to make their marriages more solid.

The intended audience of this study would be active duty, reserve, and National Guard military members and their spouses. We also recognize that others who work with and for the military—DOD teachers or civilian employees, for example—would also benefit from the study.

Most people today enter into marriage with little idea of how to make the relationship work. If they happen to be in the military, they routinely face challenges that put an incredible strain on their relationship, such as

- extended separations from spouses and families,
- long duty hours,
- fear for loved ones who may be in dangerous situations,
- moving frequently to unfamiliar environments, and
- overseas assignments.

Leader qualifications

Leading a HomeBuilders group does not require an expert Bible teacher or even a couple with a "perfect" marriage. The leader of the group is a facilitator, not a lecturer. The main function of the facilitator is to provide an environment of openness, warmth, and acceptance.

The facilitator is a fellow member of the group who has the added responsibility of guiding the group in the right direction within the limited time period. The best leaders are couples willing to share their successes and weaknesses while trying to foster a better marriage at the same time.

If you are unsure about your ability to lead, consider co-leading with another couple. You can divide the responsibilities. Together you can trust God to work in your lives and to help other couples.

Starting a HomeBuilders group

As a couple, commit to each other and to God to make the HomeBuilders group a priority for the time it will take to complete the study. (Remember, it only requires a short-term commitment. You may choose to meet weekly or every other week.) Decide how you will share responsibility for organizing and leading the group, preparing for the session, phone calling, and details of hospitality.

Inviting couples to participate

If you have attended a Military Marriage Conference or Seminar, consider asking other couples who attended to join your group. You may also want to ask your chaplain if he knows of any couples who would be interested and if you could promote the group within the chapel (see below). Invite friends, neighbors, co-workers, and parents from your children's school or teams. A personal invitation is always best.

This study also can be used in Gateway Ministries as young men and women prepare for military duty. It would be appropriate for senior cadets at academies as they look toward their first assignment and possibly marriage. Engaged couples living in the United States or overseas who are considering joining the military would also benefit.

We should mention that the content is designed primarily for couples who do not know much about the Bible. Couples who are already mature in their Christian faith may find the content very basic; we advise them to see the group as an opportunity to reach out and help couples who are younger in the faith.

Show potential group members the materials and tell them about the discussion format. You will want to assure couples that the study will help make a good marriage better, and that they will be making a limited time commitment.

An ideal size for the group is four to seven couples (including you and your spouse).

Starting HomeBuilders in your chapel

If you are interested in starting HomeBuilders in your chapel, volunteer to lead a group there. Make it clear to your chaplain that you will do the work, and show him the HomeBuilders promotional and study material. (Contact FamilyLife for other available HomeBuilders information.)

Explain how the principles from the study have affected your life, and share how chapels can use HomeBuilders in a variety of ways. But if the chaplain is not interested, respect his wishes and start a neighborhood group instead.

Small groups

Chapels most frequently use HomeBuilders studies in small groups or as an evening Bible study. If small groups already exist at your chapel, talk with the person who makes decisions on the curriculum. If there are no small groups currently meeting, you could offer to organize the first group.

Retreats or weekend emphasis

A chapel or Sunday school class often sets aside a weekend to emphasize strong marriages. This provides a great setting to share a series of HomeBuilders sessions.

Sunday school

There are two important adaptations that will need to be made if you want to use this study in a classroom setting:

1. The material you cover will need to focus on the content from the Blueprints section of each session. Blueprints is the heart of each session and is designed to last sixty minutes.

2. Most Sunday school classes are geared around a teaching format instead of a small-group format. If this study is to be used in a class setting, the class will need to adapt to a small-group dynamic. This will involve an interactive, discussion-based format, and may also require a class to break into multiple smaller groups. (We recommend groups of six to eight people.)

Promotion: Consider the following ideas:

- Advertise in base newspapers, at Family Support centers, and through command channels.

- Send invitations to chapel members and neighbors.

- Advertise in the chapel bulletin, newsletter, or flyers.

- Conduct an introductory meeting to demonstrate the effectiveness and fun of HomeBuilders.

- Have your chaplain endorse HomeBuilders from the pulpit.

- Use sign-up sheets.

- Invite your chaplain or Sunday school teacher to observe an existing class.

Childcare

It is important that your group focus on the study material without distractions and interruptions. Ask your group what works best for them. Childcare must be dependable. Some

couples will not be able to commit to every group session if
childcare is not provided. Here are some suggestions:

- Arrange babysitting in one house and hold the study in
  another.
- Pool resources to hire a babysitter.
- Ask if any couples have older children who would babysit.
- Use available childcare or chapel facilities when the nursery
  is already scheduled to be open.
- Hold your group meetings at the same time as chapel Awana
  or other children's programs.

Leading a HomeBuilders group

Before you begin each session, agree as a couple how much
you will communicate about your own marriage. Sharing openly
will help others apply biblical truths to their own lives. Study
the leader's notes and pray regularly for your group. Also,
discuss as a couple your leadership responsibilities for each
session.

It is also important to practice hospitality. Making friends is
a key to creating an environment in which God will change
lives. In our impersonal world, many couples are hungry for
friendships. God will use your relationships in an atmosphere of
mild accountability to encourage couples to apply the lessons to
their lives.

Starting the session

Share the following ground rules at the beginning of the first
session, and review them as needed:

- Share nothing that will embarrass your spouse.
- You may pass on any question.
- Anything shared in the group stays in the group.
- Couples should complete the HomeBuilders Project
  with their spouses between each session.

Simply read through the questions to lead the study. At first, you may need to wait for answers. Don't jump in too quickly with your own ideas. Naturally, couples will wait for you to answer, and by doing so, you will end up teaching the material without their input. Ideas you can solicit from the group will mean more to the participants than those you "teach." When discussion lasts too long or gets off the subject, just read the next question to stay on track.

Components of each session

Warm Up (15 minutes)

The purpose of Warm Up is to help people unwind from a busy day and get to know each other better. The questions also lead them toward the topic of that session.

Blueprints (60 minutes)

This is the heart of the study. In this category, people answer pertinent questions related to the topic of study and look to God's Word for understanding.

Wrap Up (15 minutes)

This section serves to "bring home the point" and wind down a session in an appropriate fashion.

HomeBuilders Project (60 minutes)

This is the unique application step in a HomeBuilders study. Before your meeting ends, couples are encouraged to "Make a Date" to complete this project with their spouse before the next meeting. Encourage couples to make this a priority—it will make the HomeBuilders experience twice as effective.

Additional tips

1. Keep the focus on what the Scripture says. When someone disagrees with the Scripture, affirm him for wrestling with the issue and point out that some biblical statements are hard to understand or accept. Encourage him to keep an open mind on the issue at least through the remainder of the sessions.

2. Avoid labeling an answer as "wrong"—doing so can kill the atmosphere for discussion. Encourage a person who gives a wrong or incomplete answer to look again at the question or the scripture being explored. Offer a comment such as, "That's really close" or "There's something else we need to see there." Or ask others in the group to respond.

3. Your best resource for communicating with others is your own life and marriage. Be prepared to get the discussion going by sharing things from your own lives. But as a couple, be sure that you agree beforehand about the issues and experiences you will share.

4. One thing to watch is the possibility of people in the group using the discussion as an opportunity to focus too much on their perceived shortcomings of the military. Though many questions call for couples to discuss the pressures they face in marriage because of the military lifestyle, encourage them to avoid getting sidetracked into "military bashing."

5. Take time during each session to encourage couples to work on the HomeBuilders Project before you meet again. These projects are a vital part of the HomeBuilders experience.

Praying in the group

An important part of a small group is prayer. However, as the leader you need to be sensitive to the level of comfort the people in your group have toward praying in front of others. Never call on people to pray aloud if you don't know if they are comfortable doing this. There are a number of creative approaches you can take, such as modeling prayer yourself, calling for volunteers, and letting people state their prayers in the form of finishing a sentence. A tool that is helpful in a group is a prayer list. You should lead the prayer time, but allow another couple in the group the opportunity to create, update, and distribute prayer lists as a ministry to the group.

Refreshments

Many groups choose to have refreshments because they help create an environment of fellowship. Here are a couple of suggestions:

- For the first session (or two) you should provide the refreshments and then allow the group to be involved by having a sign-up sheet.

- Consider starting your group with a short time of informal fellowship and refreshments (15 minutes), then move into the study. This way if a couple is late, they only miss the food and don't disrupt the study.

Building new leadership

As you lead, look for potential leaders who might multiply your group into new groups. Someone may even express interest in leading. Here are a few pointers to help you build new leaders:

- Look for others who demonstrate availability, teachability, and faithfulness.

- Select a couple in your group who demonstrates maturity in their Christian walk and marriage, and whom you feel would be good discussion leaders. Challenge them to lead.

- Invite them to try out the leadership role by asking one or two questions, by leading part of the session, and then leading an entire session by the end of the study.

- Challenge them to start a group after the current study is completed.

Leader's Notes

Here are some additional notes about various Blueprints questions and possible answers, if you should get stuck. The numbers below correspond to the Blueprints question numbers. Notes are not included for every question. Most questions are designed to help you make sure group members understand the correct biblical principles.

Many of the questions in this study are designed so group members can draw from their own opinions and experiences. If you share any of these points, be sure to do so in a manner that does not stifle discussion by making you the authority with the final answers. Begin your comments by saying things like, "One thing I notice in this passage is . . ." or "I think another reason for this is . . ."

Session One

Question #1: The military lifestyle offers opportunities for travel and adventures that most other families would not have. These experiences can build positive memories. Separations, although painful, can strengthen a relationship. Shared adversity can build a common bond.

Question #2: Separations due to deployments, field exercises, and temporary duty cause strain on any relationship. The need for communication increases. Permanent moves (PCS) cause strain due to having to say goodbye to old friends, make new friends, and learn a new area.

Question #3: Leaving your parents means making your relationship with your spouse your top priority. Your marriage relationship should come before your relationship with your parents. This means moving dependency for emotional, financial, and spiritual support from one's parents to one's spouse. For some couples, it is difficult to place the needs of a spouse ahead of parents' needs, and for some parents it is difficult to let their child go—not just physically, but emotionally.

Question #4: Sometimes people allow other relationships—with family or friends—to become more important. Or they allow work and career to be top priority. It's also common to be more committed to entertainment, self-fulfillment, leisure activities, or hobbies. Eventually, these other priorities can cause you to experience isolation from your spouse.

Question #6: Marriage is the first institution God created, and it is a foundation of society. God knows the damage that happens in divorce. It hurts people emotionally, and it destroys families. And when families are destroyed, the culture suffers.

Question #7: This mindset will give couples a different perspective on the inevitable problems, conflicts, and pressures they will face in marriage. They view these as issues to work through rather than issues that may cause them to grow apart.

Question #8: Abram likely had to leave his livelihood and his life as he knew it behind as he ventured forth in obedience to God.

Question #9: With a life change ahead, Abram surely felt sadness and grief as he left friends and family behind. He was probably anxious about moving into an unknown future. He may have felt excitement about the adventure ahead—but he also felt fear, frustration, and worry. To deal with these emotions, Abram turned to God in prayer, and Sarai trusted in her husband's faith.

Question #10: Separation—permanent and temporary—is part of the job. Have a positive attitude and support one another, and trust God that this new assignment comes from Him. Let the move draw you closer to each other as you anticipate a new adventure.

Question #11: Commitment is necessary in order to survive the stresses of multiple moves.

Session Two

Question #1: Lack of communication. Unmet needs. Desire to "protect" each other.

Question #3: Couples don't want to raise an issue that can't be resolved before they go. They feel guilty about rocking the boat, and are caught in the demands of preparing to deploy.

Question #7: These passages talk of living in humility and peace with one another and putting the needs of others ahead of your own. This is critical for a married couple because selfishness can quickly destroy a marriage.

Question #9: You would be thinking of what your spouse needs to talk about, and you would be willing to do it.

Session Three

Question #1: Typical problems include: not having money, little training or discipline in managing money, poor communication about bills and money while deployed, going into debt, and not having a team approach to handling finances. A lack of a team approach leads to big problems during deployment.

Here are some follow-up questions you can use to spark further discussion if you wish:

- How can handling two bank accounts cause financial challenges when a couple is separated due to deployment?
- Why do you think many couples report that the week before receiving a paycheck is often marked by stress and conflict?

Question #2: Fifty percent of the wisdom that God gave us resides in our spouse. When we fail to access that wisdom, we will cause resentment and a sense of helplessness in our spouse. This deteriorates oneness. It also can lead to overspending by one person, unexpected bills, and debt.

Question #5: Romans 13:6–8 speaks of our obligation to pay our bills, pay taxes, and stay out of debt. 1 Timothy 5:8 instructs us to provide for our relatives and family. Proverbs 3:9 tells us to give back to the Lord from what He has provided for us. Proverbs 6:6–9, 11 encourages us to save for future needs.

Question #6: Our culture continually leads us in the opposite direction. We are encouraged to spend money on things we don't need. We're encouraged to go into debt.

Question #7: Occasionally, you may need to borrow money to provide food, housing, and transportation for your family. But debt should be avoided wherever possible. A mortgage and car loan should be paid off in advance when possible.

Question #8: Greed (materialism), coveting, and the desire for instant gratification cause many people to go into excessive debt to satisfy themselves.

Question #9: These passages all speak of the dangers of borrowing money. Borrowing money is not forbidden in the Bible, but it is strongly discouraged. The borrower is servant to the lender. Don't get into debt unless you have the means to pay.

Question #11: Couples who succeed financially usually communicate before and during a deployment about what bills are due, how much money is being spent, and how much is being saved. They have a plan on how to manage their money, and they stick with the plan.

Session Four

Question #1: George was exposing himself to temptation through pornography, and he was not controlling his thoughts. Both he and Judy are opening themselves up to emotional attachments to others, and this leads them to begin comparing their spouse to others.

Question #2: They need to avoid things that tempt them. George could join or start a Bible study and be accountable to some other Christian men. He could maintain good communication with his wife by e-mail, phone calls, or love letters. He could have her picture always in the open.

Question #3: Spend time in Bible study and prayer daily. Memorize and meditate on appropriate Bible verses. Be accountable to other people of the same sex. Maintain close communication with each other. Don't read or watch tempting material. Avoid compromising situations. Talk in advance with your accountability partner about potential situations. Pray for each other.

Question #4: You are not alone in your temptation. God will always provide a way to escape or to stand up to temptation if you are willing to trust Him. This applies to all temptation in life, including the sexual temptation you may face while apart.

Question #5: Defense: God sees what we do, and we will suffer the consequences of our actions.

Question #6: Defense: Running from temptation means turning away from any situation that would tempt you.

Sometimes this means averting your eyes when you see an image inadvertently—while passing by a magazine newsstand, for example. It also means avoiding books, magazines, movies, television shows, and websites that tempt you to look at suggestive images.

Offense: Pursuing the good things—righteousness, faith, hope, love, etc.—means filling your mind and your time with things that draw you closer to God. Do this with others who are heading in the same direction as you are.

Question #7: Knowing how easy it is to be tempted, we should encourage each other toward purity.

Question #8: Accountability can help us avoid sin. If you are on deployment, for example, knowing that your partner is going to ask, "Did you read any pornography while you were gone?" will motivate you to avoid it. Knowing that someone will be asking us questions about our behavior, our attitudes, and our thought life should motivate us to be more diligent in areas we struggle in.

MILITARY Marriage SEMINARS

Get away with your spouse for a special weekend focused on strengthening your marriage. You'll hear from speakers who not only know the challenges of a military marriage, but can offer practical solutions with a solid, biblical foundation.

You will have uninterrupted time with your spouse, giving you an opportunity to understand one another and apply what you've learned.

During the weekend you'll:

- Understand God's design for marriage

- Develop teamwork in marriage by understanding biblical roles

- Identify forces that destroy intimacy

- Resolve conflict in relationships

- Achieve deeper levels of intimacy

For more information about Military Marriage Seminars in your area, visit www.MilitaryMinistry.org and click on Military Families > Military Marriage Seminars.